Web-Based Startups

WEB-BASED STARTUPS:

THE 21 THINGS EVERY ENTREPRENEUR NEEDS TO KNOW ABOUT WEB DESIGN AND INTERNET MARKETING

PAUL J. SCOTT

Cover & Book Design by Nikki Ward, Morrison Alley Design

Although the author and publisher have made every effort to ensure the accuracy and completeness of information contained in this book, we assume no responsibility for errors, inaccuracies, omissions, or any inconsistency herein. Any slights of people, places, or organizations are unintentional.

First Printing 2016

ISBN 978-0-9966874-2-3

Table of Contents

Introduction

Introduction: What Makes Web-Based Startups Different?

Starting a business is kind of a big deal. What begins as a simple idea can turn into a healthy side project, an income-producing passion, or even a way to change your life and the lives of others.

I know, because I haven't just built my own business from scratch; I've helped hundreds of other entrepreneurs to do it, too. My company, GoingClear Interactive, started with an inspiration, many cups of coffee, and a lot of late nights spent at my laptop.

Since then, my business has grown, and I've gotten the chance to work with several different successful entrepreneurs, some of whom came into the game with a minimum of free time or spare cash and some that already had a business that they wanted to create a new online revenue model for. They have all shared something, though – in each case, it has been an absolute thrill to watch their brand-new ventures go from a vague concept into a growing, exciting enterprise.

Believe me when I tell you there's nothing better than reaching that *this could actually work* moment. It makes all the brainstorming, strategizing, and budgeting worth it.

Of course, there are a lot of things that have to come before that epiphany, and one of the biggest involves actually planning and launching a successful website. That's true for any new company that wants to open its doors in the digital age, but it's especially critical for web-based startups.

What is a web-based startup? I'm glad you asked. It's a business that's being built and developed around a website concept. In other words, it means the website is the business, or at least the public-facing part of the company (you may still have factories, warehouses, offices, etc., behind the scenes).

There are thousands of successful web-based companies, and you probably use dozens of them every week. Amazon, eBay, and Zappos.com are all good examples, as are Expedia, Yelp, and Google. A web-based startup is just the earliest version of this kind of business, whether it's a side project being run from someone's home or a full-blown business that's being backed by serious venture capital.

If you're planning to launch a new business that's dependent on a website or web interface, this is the perfect book for you. That's because I'm going to use my experience as an entrepreneur and web developer to show you everything you need to know in order to get your website (and company) up and running quickly and profitably.

However, if you are launching a startup that isn't web-based, don't put this book or the tablet you're reading it on down just yet. Although some of the ideas and examples I will give are specific to web-based companies, the underlying principles apply to *all* startups.

The fact of the matter is that all brand-new businesses face a lot of the same hurdles, regardless of whether they are based on HTML code or a Main Street retail location. Startups need to generate marketing and branding concepts from nothing, to announce themselves to a base of customers that doesn't even know they exist, and to go from zero to positive cash flow as quickly as possible.

At the same time, startups are usually driven by the vision and enthusiasm of an entrepreneur (or an entrepreneurial team), and tend to be more progressive and flexible than existing companies while having the ability to act on impulses or ideas more quickly than established firms.

Put all of this together and you have the makings of something that's fast, exciting, and full of potential. In the coming chapters – organized as stand-alone topics that you can read back to front or refer to individually as needed – I'm going to fill you in on the key topics and hurdles that will make or break your new web-based startup.

As you read them, remember that the advice I'm giving you is based on practical experience. You won't find any "fluff," or general ideas that don't apply to the matter at hand. Instead of weighing this book down with theory and counterpoints, I'm going to share with you the ideas that actually work and then trust you to put them to good use. Believe me when I tell you that you're going to be too busy to waste time on what doesn't matter, so I'll distill the most important facts down to the essentials.

If that sounds good to you, let's get started!

1 | Your Website Is A First (And Sometimes Only) Point Of Contact

At one point in history, you could begin a business by hanging out a shingle, literally, and letting the world know you are open to customers and clients. These days, things get a little more complicated. Starting most businesses will require, at a minimum, a license, a bank account, and some sort of marketing plan.

And, perhaps most importantly of all, it requires a website.

Although this is a book about web-based startups, I should point out that the need for a website applies to almost any kind of venture that's bigger than a weekend vegetable stand. If you want people to find you, you need an online presence. That's because, more often than not, your website is going to be your first and only point of contact.

Think about that for just a second. In those long-gone days I mentioned a moment ago, an entrepreneur could get by with networking, word-of-mouth advertising, or just meeting new people on the street. And, until recently, a business could get by with the right kind of print or media advertising, a good location, and some combination of low prices and a strong reputation.

In the digital age, though, you can still do all of those things very well and fail. Why? Because people are going to double-check everything you say – and compare you to your competitors – within minutes by going onto the Internet. A lot of us won't even visit a restaurant down the street without seeing what kinds of reviews it has on Yelp.

This is obviously even more pertinent for web-based startups. For these kinds of companies, the website isn't just the hub of customer interaction; it's the entirety of your public-facing business. Things like pricing and customer service are only as valuable as they are visible. If it's not on the website, people aren't going to find out about it.

That leads us to some interesting insights and conclusions, which I'll get to in a second. However, it's *also* something you should remember as you move through the rest of this book. It doesn't matter how strong your concept is, or how passionate you are about your new business, if your website isn't up to the task. It has to be your salesperson, your customer service agent, your PR representative, and your chief recruiter. Your website *is* the business.

With that out of the way, let's get a little bit deeper and think about what makes for a great startup website...

First Impressions Matter

A web-based startup enters the market with a couple of disadvantages. First, the business doesn't have a long history of service or reputation to draw on. So, it's only natural for buyers to be a little skeptical (or even wonder if the business is legitimate at all). That's true for any brand-new company, of course, but as a web entrepreneur sometimes you don't have the luxury of meeting customers face-to-face.

Additionally, your closest competitors are just a click away, even if they are geographically distant. That means you might be compared to other companies customers already know and like, even if you aren't in the same particular niche within your market.

The answer to both of these challenges is to instantly win buyers over with credibility. And you can only do that by making a strong first impression with a professionally designed website.

As humans, we make snap judgments about whether we can trust a source of information or not. A lot of what goes into those decisions basically comes down to how well-presented the ideas and promises are. A strong web design can go a long, long way toward reducing skepticism and building trust in the minds of first-time visitors.

Your Website Should Pass The Eyeball Test

Along with making your business seem credible and professional, your website should be able to pass what I call the "eyeball test." That means information isn't just clean and organized, but it's also relevant.

For instance, when someone visits your website for the first time, they should be able to tell – in a couple of seconds or less – who you are, what your company is all about, whom your products or services are meant for, and why buyers should be interested in working with you instead of someone else.

If that sounds like a tall order, then know that it is. But without having that kind of information up-front and easy to find, you're going to lose some customers who don't immediately grasp what your business is all about. Remember, those first few seconds matter a lot, and you need to make the most of them by building credibility and making the case for your web-based startup.

Usability Is Key

If customers can't find what they're looking for on a website, and especially one they aren't familiar with, they will almost always take their time, attention, and money elsewhere. That's why usability, which is simply the science of making your website clean, simple, and easy to navigate, is such a big deal for startups.

Good usability really comes down to clear layouts, easy-to-read fonts, and lots of search and navigation tools that seem intuitive. In other words, it's having a clean interface that visitors can "catch on to" immediately and find what they're looking for without becoming frustrated or annoyed.

It can be easy to go overboard with design features on a startup website, especially when you want to impress visitors that you are hoping will become long-term buyers. But you should never sacrifice usability for aesthetics, because a website that's easy to navigate is more valuable to customers than one with an unorthodox design.

Don't Let Your Startup Website Be An Afterthought

The idea that having a good website is crucial for a web-based startup seems obvious, but some entrepreneurs get so excited about the concept that they either rush through the design and development process or don't budget the appropriate amount of time and money to their most valuable business asset.

The quality of your website will likely make or break your new business, so make it a centerpiece of your strategy and do everything you can to ensure that the final product is exactly what you need.

2 | Domain Names Matter

Realtors and veteran entrepreneurs will tell you that location is *everything*. What you might not realize is that the old axiom is as true online as it is in the real world.

In the world of web-based startups, your "real estate" is your company's domain name. It's what people have to remember to type in if they want to return to your website, or to tell a friend or colleague about your business. While some customers will undoubtedly find you through search engines and social media, and others will bookmark a page on your website, having a good domain name is still important, especially as you look to build a sense of awareness and recognition about your venture.

Knowing that, let's take a closer look at some of the things that make a domain name valuable...

A Great Startup Domain Name Should Make Sense

Because prime real estate is a precious thing on the web, it's become harder and harder to snag great domain names over the years. As a result, you see lots of startups using made-up words, or nonsensical phrases, as their domains.

This is a strategy that *can* work, but it's probably going to end up costing you a little bit extra in terms of raising public awareness since it won't be immediately apparent what you do. Sometimes, a good trade-off can be to choose something innovative that has a vague association to your business. As an obvious example, I chose *GoingClear Interactive* because it represented my business philosophy, but also because the domain name was available.

The Best Domain Names Are Memorable

Not only should your domain name ideally bear some relation to the products or services you plan to offer, but it should be something memorable so new customers can remember it when they want to return.

eBay didn't necessarily mean anything when the company was first begun, but it had a certain ring to it and was something users could recall. The same goes for Google, which had a scientific meaning but wasn't in the everyday vernacular.

Likewise, Yelp was a rarely used word before the website came along.

As you can tell from those examples, choosing something memorable can be a big key to the success of your startup. Just know that the farther your domain name is from your actual business, the more time (and possibly money) you'll have to spend getting people to understand what you do.

Your Domain Should Be Easy To Spell

Remember, one of the first things you have to do as an entrepreneur is build up a base of customers who come back to your website and business again and again. They won't do so if they aren't able to remember and accurately spell your domain name.

This is a minor point, but it can get to be a big issue if you don't think about things up-front. Never forget that most newspapers are written to a seventh-grade level because they need to have public appeal. If there is something in your domain name that's likely to be misspelled again and again, look for a better option elsewhere.

Shorter Domains Are Better Than Longer Ones

This is related to the last two points. If you want people to remember your domain, and type it in frequently, then shorter is better than longer. Entrepreneurs are sometimes tempted to grab lengthy domain names (those with three or four words used together) because they seem like the best available, but you should try to keep yours shorter.

The very best startup domains are one or two words, and don't contain any dashes or hyphens. If you can find one of these (and one that fits the criteria above), you're off to a great start.

Domain Names Have Big Search Engine Optimization Implications

If you are considering launching a new web-based startup, or have one already, then you probably don't need me to tell you that Google and the other search engines can be a huge source of new business. What a lot of entrepreneurs don't realize, though, is that Google actually places a great deal of weight on domain names when determining search results.

Although it's obviously just one factor in search engine optimization, it will be easier to promote your website if important search keywords can be found in your domain name. In fact, you might use those as a good starting point when brainstorming possibilities.

Domain Name Extensions Are (Slowly) Expanding

Since the first days of Internet marketing, the goal for any web entrepreneur has been to secure a domain name with a ".com" extension. There have been other choices for years – namely ".net" and ".org" – but these have been largely seen as second-best alternatives by a wide margin.

Now, with lots of new domain extensions coming to the market, things are opening up a bit. But it's important to remember that even though lots of extensions are now available, they aren't nearly as memorable. So ideally you'll still want to find an open ".com" if you can. And, once you do, you should grab the other extensions so no one else registers them later and ends up poaching your traffic.

Should You Buy A Domain Name?

The chances are good that, somewhere in your search for available domain names, you'll come across a possibility you really like, even though it has already been registered by someone else (either for their own use or as a "premium domain" investment). Should you consider making an offer to buy it?

Obviously, there are pros and cons, and a lot depends on how many different viable choices you have to work with. Paying big money for a domain takes away from your startup budget, of course, but having the right online real estate can make or break your company.

Our best advice? Consider the options (and budget) both ways, and see what kinds of sacrifices you'll have to make in other areas of your company to purchase the domain. You don't want to break the bank, or remove key features from your website, just to get the right URL. If you can afford it, though, purchasing the right domain can be a great investment that pays you back time and time again.

You don't just need a great website; you need it to be at the right address. So don't overlook the value of having a great domain, and don't settle for one that won't help your business grow.

3 | You Don't Need A Good Web Design Partner... You Need A Great One

If your web-based startup needs a great web presence to get noticed and become a profitable enterprise, then your first task – right after developing a great concept for your startup – should be finding the right web design and development team to work with.

A quick search on Google will give you dozens and dozens of *options*, but not necessarily many *answers*. In fact, even a referral from a trusted friend or advisor might not be enough. That's partially because there are so many web design and development companies out there (I should know, we compete against them every day). It's also because there isn't a "perfect" web designer, just the one that's the right fit for your project.

In other words, the best fit for another client might not be the right one for you. Things like design style, location, budget, and industry expertise might all factor in.

However, there are a handful of things that great web design companies have in common. Here is a short list of the attributes you really need to find...

Your Web Designer Should Have Great Design Instincts

Because the look and layout of your website are going to be so important, you want to choose a partner that has great design instincts. In other words, to work with someone who can generate attractive pages that will impress potential customers.

Surprising as it might seem, there are a lot of web design teams who are great with things like coding and programming, but not as strong with the visual aspects of web design. Don't settle for a company that can't give you the professional look you're striving for.

You Want A Web Design Team That Can Handle Development

Of course, there are two sides of the coin when it comes to working on the web. A website doesn't just have to be beautiful, but functional. In my first book, I explained the process of web development for non-programmers. Although most business owners and executives don't spend much time thinking about web development, it factors heavily into their online success.

Simply put, your website can't just look pretty – aesthetics are important, but it also needs the right programming to help you offer unique features, automate key tasks, and cut costs. Don't trust your startup website to a design team that doesn't handle web programming, as well.

Your Web Designer Should Know Your Business (Or Get To Know It)

Within the realm of web design, industry experience is somewhat overblown. Just because someone designed pages for one of your colleagues or competitors doesn't mean they'll do a great job for you. In fact, they may come into the project with some unnecessary assumptions.

But while you don't necessarily need a web designer who has already worked with a company like yours, you do want one that will take the time to get to know what your business is all about. Great web designers emphasize the discovery process so they can highlight your most important features and benefits.

Your Web Designer Should Have Great Design Instincts

Because the look and layout of your website are going to be so important, you want to choose a partner that has great design instincts. In other words, to work with someone who can generate attractive pages that will impress potential customers.

But while you don't necessarily need a web designer who has already worked with a company like yours, you *do* want one that will take the time to get to know what your business is all about. Great web designers emphasize the discovery process so they can highlight your most important features and benefits.

Look For The Right Portfolio And Project History

Most business people, when evaluating different web design companies, start by looking at portfolios to see if they like the finished pages from a visual point of view. That's important, but don't forget to go a little deeper.

When evaluating different web designers, you also want to look at case studies, testimonials, and project histories. In particular, you want to see whether a web design team has finished projects on time, been easy to work with, and stayed within budget. Even more importantly, you want to know whether former clients have seen a positive return on investment from their websites or not.

It's easy to be distracted by nice visuals you see in online portfolios, but remember that results are what will make your project a success or failure in the end.

Remember That Size Matters When Choosing Web Design Partners

The size of your web design team could be an important consideration. It's not that there's a right or wrong size for a creative team to be, just that there are important advantages and disadvantages to consider.

For example, a solo designer is likely to charge you the lowest rates because they have very little in the way of overhead expenses. However, they may also have limited availability and expertise. You're stuck with whatever skills they have as an individual, and may find yourself waiting a long time for your website to be finished if they become distracted by another project or personal issues.

Large web design companies, on the other hand, tend to run like clockwork. They will likely have several different teams of designers and coders who can help you out. But it goes without saying that you're also going to be paying for those big, expensive offices, along with their advertising, support staff, and extensive sales and advertising campaigns. So while you'll get great service, it will probably be expensive (and possibly impersonal, if your work is passed from one designer or employee to another).

The best answer, for a lot of clients, is to work with a small to medium-sized web design team that has consistent leadership, talented web designers, and a personal touch. With that kind of company, you can know what you're getting, and skip the huge overhead costs associated with giant advertising firms.

Look For A Web Designer That Knows And Loves Startups

As I mentioned in the opening of this book, startups are a whole different category of business. New companies have unique needs, especially when it comes to budgets, timing, and web development.

Getting a startup moving from scratch is a big job, and a big challenge. Choose a web design and development partner that understands the scope of the project, and is excited to help you get your brand-new business up and running.

The bottom line is this: When it comes to choosing the right web designer to help your startup come to life, having a creative team that's good just isn't enough. You need a partner who is great. Your goal should be to find the design or development company that can take your vision, turn it into reality, and help you find success online.

Without the right creative group, you're going to have a hard time generating any traction with your new company. So, choose very carefully.

4 | Know The Difference Between Web Design And Web Development

The look of your startup website matters a great deal, and first impressions can make or break a brand-new business. However, your website also needs to have some power "under the hood" if it's going to be useful for visitors and customers. That's where web development comes into play.

A lot of entrepreneurs don't understand the difference between web design and web development. This is helped by the fact that many in our industry use the two terms interchangeably. Also, the lines between them tend to blur when you get into the actual business of drawing and scripting pages.

However, for the sake of simplicity, let's use a straightforward definition that's easy to understand: *Web design affects the way your new site looks; web development has to do with programming, and determines what capabilities your site will have.*

So if you're looking at the homepage of a website and seeing graphics, pictures, and text, that's all basic web design. If you're using it to see whether products are in stock, to place an online order, or to add your name to a database or distribution list, that's web development.

Again, these differences are subtle. But as the owner of a web-based startup, it matters that you can identify the distinction, and that you choose a vendor who can give you great work when it comes to both design and development. Otherwise, you might just choose a creative partner who has a decent portfolio and a low price, while ignoring a few important aspects of your new web presence.

To get a sense for why web development needs to be central to your startup strategy, let's take a closer look at the details...

Web Development Has Many Business Uses

Whereas web design can be used to present a business in the best possible light, web development can be used for automation, list management, marketing, and e-commerce. It gives entrepreneurs easy ways to generate more money, spend less, and save time.

These are all important advantages for any company, but for brand-new businesses they are especially important. A web-based startup, for example, might not have the funds to hire a big customer service team. What they can do, though, is use a series of databases and manage interactions to let buyers update account information, process orders, and even handle returns or FAQs.

By making the most of web development, you can introduce new ideas to an industry. You can also find ways to make the most of your investment by reaching more customers and providing them with better service... all while lowering costs.

Web Development Brings Out Innovative Ideas

Some of the biggest and most successful web-based startups began with ideas about what websites might be able to do. Companies like Amazon, eBay, Google, and Expedia were all just once possibilities envisioned on the back of a napkin.

While web design and online marketing are undoubtedly important to their success, it's development that really made the ideas fly. Without a searchable database and bidding system, eBay would just be a set of online advertisements. If it were missing revolutionary search, pricing, shipping, and recommendation software models, Amazon would be a simple e-commerce site. And of course, Expedia relies on integration between lots of different airlines, hotels, and reservation systems just to be useful.

Web design is the packaging, but web programming can add real power to your new site. Very often, that's what will keep customers coming back for more.

The Web Development Process Is A Bit Different

Web design and web development both follow a similar process, but there are important differences. In particular, while a design team may be free to move forward with an idea after getting your feedback, programmers and developers heavily emphasize testing before a new site is launched.

A good website – and the web apps that run its core features – will have to interact fluently with a number of different computers and browsers, including smartphones and tablets. Any inconsistency, or outright incompatibility, can lead to a poor user experience. Or worse, they can open you up to unstable websites and online security issues.

In order to make sure that your website will have the right look *and* functionality, it's beneficial to have a design and development team that are used to working closely together. In other words, you'll want to avoid a web design company that outsources development one project at a time, if possible.

Designers and developers are used to working together, and working in similar ways. There are important differences in how they get things done, though, and those can have a big effect on the finished project.

Web Development Can Make Or Break Your Startup

I don't want to undersell the value of great web design, because first impressions matter a great deal when you're trying to convince people that your new business is credible and trustworthy. But what your new website can actually do will ultimately determine whether you can stay in business and turn a profit.

Without the right web development, your pages won't have the kind of functionality you need to stand out in the market. And without the right web developer, the coding and testing process might not be rigorous enough to spot issues or errors before it's too late.

When your website crashes, has incomplete features, or doesn't live up to its promises, your new business is in trouble. If at all possible, you should choose a web designer who understands startups, produces great visuals, and can handle custom web development. The combination of those skills can easily make or break your business in the first few months.

For more information on this important topic, check out my book *Building a Successful Web App: A Businessperson's Guide To Making Your Website Do More*. It's a short guide that walks you step by step through the process of envisioning and creating a website with real business functionality. And make sure you don't overlook the importance of development as you launch your new startup.

5 | Every Startup Needs A Responsive Website

When you're trying to build a web-based startup, it goes without saying that web design and development are important. But there is one particular part of the process that deserves special mention (and is overlooked far too often). That involves making sure your new website is *responsive*.

Responsive web technology went from being a "new idea" to "best practice" in an incredibly short period of time, even by Internet industry standards. In a business where we constantly argue over which concepts or trends are here to stay, it was something that was just so obvious and valuable that most reputable creative teams picked up on it right away.

So what exactly is responsive design, and why is it so valuable to your startup? Let me fill you in the basics...

What Is A Responsive Web Design?

A responsive website is one that can appear in different sizes and formats to adjust to various screen dimensions. It will display one way on a traditional laptop or desktop computer, for example, and a different way on a smartphone or tablet. It "responds" to the size and platform a visitor is using, hence the term *responsive*.

It's important to note that responsive websites aren't even fixed to devices or screen sizes. You can adjust the size of a window on a large desktop monitor, for instance, and still see the presentation of a specific webpage change as a result. The responsive elements are coded directly into the underlying HTML, so users (i.e., your customers) don't have to do anything special to take advantage of it.

Why Responsive Technology Is So Important

Responsive web design is cool, but that's not why it suddenly became so popular and valuable. Instead, it has been the explosion of web-ready mobile devices that is driving the trend.

Around the middle of 2014, mobile users started to outnumber "traditional" computer users on the web in North America. Even though most people use a mixture of desktop or laptop computers, tablets, and smartphones, there are more people viewing the web on smaller screens at any given moment than there are computer users surfing the Internet.

That notion would have been unimaginable just a few years ago. But mobile computing caught on quickly, and businesses had to find a way to keep up. Although some companies have used (and continue to use) a mobile-specific version of their websites, implementing a responsive web design is almost always the better choice.

Responsive vs. Mobile Websites

As an entrepreneur, you may come across a web designer who recommends a mobile version of your website instead of responsive web design. However, there is a big disadvantage to following that approach.

It's a matter of utility. Unless you happen to be attracting *millions* of mobile visitors on a weekly basis, you don't have a need for a separate and distinct version of your website.

Building and maintaining another web presence would significantly add to your startup costs, and wouldn't bring much in the way of benefits. That's especially true when you consider that one of your sites might siphon search engine traffic from the other.

Additionally, if you really had that much demand for mobile-only visits, you'd probably be better off creating a native phone app with increased security and updated features than you would investing in a mobile version of your website that could become outdated in the future.

Responsive Isn't Just About Keeping Up... It's About Getting Ahead

Because so many of your potential customers are using mobile devices, it's important that your website be compatible with their smaller screens. Besides, an outdated website without responsive functionality isn't just a huge annoyance to customers, but is also more apt to be ignored by Google.

The engineers running the world's largest search engine know just how important mobile web usage has become, and don't want to annoy their users (who ultimately are their source of revenue) by directing them toward websites that won't display correctly on small screens. So a new company that doesn't incorporate responsive web design is just asking for trouble.

Don't Launch A Brand-New Website That's Already Out Of Date

When you launch a web-based startup, the burden is on you to prove to customers your service is faster, smarter, or more efficient than the competition. Otherwise, why would they take a chance working with your company instead of shopping with the companies they already know and trust?

Launching a non-responsive website sends the wrong message. It tells buyers you aren't up to date, don't care about convenience, and want them to do things that work on your terms, not theirs.

Save yourself a ton of headaches – not to mention missed marketing opportunities – by insisting that your new website be responsive and mobile-compatible from the first minute it goes live. Your customers are already accessing the web via smartphones and tablets every day. Make sure they can use their favorite devices to work with you online.

6 | How To Get The Startup Website You Need On A Shoestring Budget

A few well-funded spinoff ventures aside, most startups begin with very limited capital. In fact, many entrepreneurs are working with personal savings, inheritances, or loans secured in their own names. That can lead to difficult, or even painful, choices when it comes to things like web design and development.

It can also be problematic when working with creative teams who don't understand the constraints startups face, since they may not pay enough attention to budget overruns.

From experience, I can tell you the best answer to these problems is a simple one: Find your MVP. It's the perfect way to get the startup website you need on a shoestring budget.

What's Your MVP?

MVP, in this context, refers to *Minimum Viable Product*. In more straightforward terms, it's the smallest version of your website that you could launch to test your concept.

A lot of entrepreneurs approach the idea of a web-based startup with the thought that they are going to include every feature, idea, and inspiration that comes to mind. Unfortunately, that tends to lead to a long development cycle, with lots of costs, testing, and setbacks. The client could even run out of money during the process without ever getting their website launched, much less advertised and promoted.

What good is it trying to do everything, if you accomplish nothing? Unless money is no object, take my advice and start small.

How To Find Your MVP

Entrepreneurs tend to think big, and that's a good thing. If you're reading this book, it's likely that you have lots and lots of different ideas about what your website will be able to do in the future, and the directions your business could expand in.

Trying to chase down all of these opportunities could quickly leave you broke, exhausted, and with a business plan that isn't coherent. Scaling things back and developing an MVP is a much better option. It saves time and money, of course, but it also lets an entrepreneur reserve a bit of cash for other parts of the project (like advertising) while giving them the chance to test the idea with the public.

Zeroing in on an MVP version of your idea is usually pretty simple. Most new web-based startups come down to a simple concept. That concept can be pared down to a smaller scope to see how well it works. For instance, you could limit the first version of a website to a few different products, target a smaller geographic area, or remove a few features and functions that you expect to include in the final product.

You don't want to strip your idea so much that it can't work, of course, but neither do you want to get caught up in the details before they become important. So ask yourself what a reduced version of your website would look like. What are a few "extras" that you could live without? Remember that you aren't giving up on your idea, just looking for the most economical way to get it off the ground.

The Benefits Of MVP Testing

The MVP lets you float an idea with a minimum of expense and waiting time. If your concept flies, you can always expand and grow. In fact, it will be easier because you'll have some recognition and revenue to work with. Alternatively, if things don't go as planned, producing an MVP gives you the option to tweak your idea – or even cut your costs – before using your entire startup budget.

Even if your website is well designed and developed, it's highly likely that you'll want to make changes to it in the weeks and months after it's been launched. Customer feedback, changing market conditions, and simple "aha" moments can all make you re-think parts of your platform or messaging. If you've already spent your time and money coming up with a finished version of your website, that can be a problem. But if you've used an MVP, you can simply add, pivot, or pursue a new inspiration.

This is particularly true when it comes to revenue model testing. Often, an entrepreneur will be sure that customers or advertisers are going to work in a certain way, when the reality turns out to be different. Suddenly, they find that they need to change their pricing structure, add new subscription options, or otherwise alter the way they receive money.

These kinds of shifts don't just affect a website, but also the associated marketing and underlying business principles. It's always a good idea to do a bit of research and testing – again, using a scaled version of your website – before you push all of your chips into the center of the table, so to speak.

Start With A Smaller Version Of Your Website

Experience working with more than a dozen startups has taught me that there is virtually no downside to beginning with an MVP version of a website or web app. It's faster and less expensive. But more importantly, it gives a new business the flexibility to grow and adapt.

No matter how great an idea is, it's always going to need a little bit of refinement once you get to market. There are some things you simply can't know until you try to go out and find customers. By using an MVP, you can make sure you still have the resources you need when it turns out your web-based startup needs a few key improvements before it can really take off.

7 | Getting Great Content For Your Startup Website

We have explored the way web design creates great first impressions, and how web development gives your pages power to actually do things that are useful. But before we get away from the topic of building and creating a website, there is one other subject we have to address: getting great web content.

Messaging matters. When visitors come to visit your new company online for the first time, the visuals they see are going to form an impression. It's the writing on your pages, however, that's going to convince them to stay, take action, and return again at a later date.

You can think of design, development, and content creation as a three-legged stool. Your website can't stand on one, or even two, of these elements. All three need to be in place before you can launch a successful business and turn a profit.

Let's take a brief look at what makes for great startup web content, and how you can get it or create it...

Great Web Content Isn't Just SEO Copy

Most business people are at least somewhat familiar with the concept of search engine optimization (SEO), along with the art of incorporating important search terms and phrases into your web content. With Google processing *billions* of search queries every day, obtaining a high search ranking can be a big boost to your business.

Although SEO is undoubtedly important to the success of your startup, it shouldn't be the focus of your web content. In order to attract customers, you need to engage them first. Jamming search phrases awkwardly into every headline or paragraph isn't a good way to do that.

Your primary goal in writing or acquiring web content should be to persuade buyers to give you a try, not see how many times you can use a particular search term.

Every Startup Should Tell A Story

Startups have a big advantage over their competitors. Namely, that customers who find them tend to be *curious*.

When someone visits your website for the first time, they don't know what your brand-new company does, or where it came from. You should use your web content to tell a story. If you do so, they won't just hang around to learn more, but may actually start to root for your business and want to see it succeed.

It's human nature to pull for the underdog. When we come across a new venture and find out that it's a labor of love, we think of our own dreams and efforts. We transfer some of our hopes on to the new discovery, and hope to see it take flight.

Your customers have enough big, faceless organizations they work with every day. They don't need to come across another company that seems generic and completely profit-driven. Use your web content to share your passion and tell a story. You'll connect with customers in a stronger way and get them thinking about how they can help your new business grow.

The Four Elements Of Great Web Content

There is a lot that goes into the finer points of web content, but generally speaking, the pages on your website need to cover four important topics: who you are, what you do, who your business is for, and what a visitor should do next.

In the first case, telling people who you are is simple enough. If your business is small, family-operated, or born out of personal passion for a certain type of industry or product, say so online. All of those show customers you care, and make web visitors trust you more.

Likewise, make it easy for anyone who visits your website to tell what you do within a few seconds or less. The more customers have to guess about what kinds of products or services they can get from you, or what your website is even about, the more likely it is that they're going to take their attention (and money) to one of your competitors.

Identifying and appealing to your target audience is a little more nuanced. Even the most popular websites aren't for everyone. Think back to our earlier examples – Amazon is built for people who like low-cost shopping and two-day delivery, Expedia appeals to budget travelers, and so on. Even within your market or industry, it's likely that some buyers are a better fit than others. Structure your content in a way that makes it easy for prospects to see whether or not they might be better off doing business with you.

And finally, always use your web content to give buyers a next step. Invite them to make a purchase, sign up for your email newsletter, or contact you for a consultation. The more inviting and encouraging your pages are, the more likely website visitors are to want to do what you ask.

Should You Write Web Content Yourself, Or Hire A Writer?

There isn't a right or wrong answer to this question. Generally speaking, a good copywriter will work more quickly than a business person can. Plus, they can help distill your marketing messages down into something that's engaging and actionable. That means more conversions over time, and a more profitable startup business.

But by writing content yourself, you can decide exactly what you want to say. After all, no one knows your business as well as you do. That is a huge benefit if you have products or services that are very technical and/or difficult to explain. In those cases, you might get a better result, and finish your web content more quickly, by simply writing on your own.

Of course, developing web content doesn't have to be an "either/or" proposition. You can always start writing your pages, or put together some notes, and then turn to an experienced writer or editor to finish them.

Don't Let Web Content Be An Afterthought

You can think of the web content on your pages as the glue that holds your site together. Your words are the piece of the puzzle that tells customers who you are, what you do, and how you can help them.

That's a big job, and a good reason why you should never treat web content as an afterthought. When people first meet your business, they aren't sure what to think. You can use great design to make a strong first impression, and web programming to offer them advanced functionality. It's only with the right content, though, that you're going to get them interested enough to take action.

8 | Use The Secret Weapon On Your Startup Website

You may not know it, but you have secret weapon on your startup company's website: the "About" page.

A lot of entrepreneurs treat this section of the website as little more than a placeholder to store a brief company description or a few press release-style bios. That's a big mistake, however, because your About page can earn you a great deal of attention, create buyer loyalty, and help you differentiate yourself from your competitors.

Let's take a look at what makes a startup "About" page so important, and how you can make the most of yours...

The Numbers Don't Lie

One of the best ways to figure out what's actually going on with a website, and what customers are responding to, is to pay close attention to web analytics. Specifically, heat maps that show where visitors look, and which pieces of content catch their eye, can be invaluable when it comes to reading buyers' minds.

As any web designer who has used these tools can tell you, About pages are among the most commonly viewed by first-time visitors to a website. What's more, searchers spend a great deal of time on them. While they might scan text about individual products or services, they will inevitably give bios and company descriptions a close read.

This shouldn't be so surprising. Everyone knows about the established companies in every industry – they've been around for a long time and have lots of advertising behind them. A startup is an unknown entity, however. It could be almost anything, and have any sort of story behind it.

When people find something new, and potentially valuable, they become curious. Don't be surprised, then, if the About page on your website is one of the most frequently visited, and one that potential customers spend a lot of time with. Use that attention wisely.

Cover The Basics

Your About page should start with a quick description of what your company is, the kinds of products and services you have to offer, and where it's located.

Not only will this help reinforce your most important marketing messages, but it will serve as an easy way to bring new prospects who come to your site up to speed. Remember that some of the people coming to your pages will be doing so because they've read about your new business somewhere, seen some of your marketing, or have been referred by another person. One of the first things they might do is visit your About page to see whether you're a good fit for what they need.

Providing some basic information about your business and what it does is good advice for any page on your website, but especially in your About description.

Tell A Story

It's worth mentioning again that your About page should be as colorful as it is accurate. Customers are naturally interested in new businesses and the stories about how they came to be. They want to know about the people involved, the reasons behind the start of the company, and what makes the venture different from other businesses that are already in the market.

If what they find on your About page reads like a corporate press release – with dry facts and figures – they have no particular reason to feel any specific way about your company. But if they know that you're hoping to make streets safer, preserve a generations-old family recipe, or bring a new technology to the public, you've given them a cause they can get behind.

Almost every entrepreneur I've ever met has a good story about why they have finally decided to take the plunge and launch their own web-based startup. Why not put those to great use?

Stories are interesting, engaging, and repeatable. Facts and details can be relevant, but stories are shared from one group and customer to the next. Use yours to bring buyers over to your side and give them a behind-the-scenes look at what makes you passionate about your business. Doing so costs you nothing, and could have far-reaching effects on your marketing campaigns.

Include Bios With Photos And Personal Trivia

Just like customers like to know more about brand-new companies, they are often intrigued by the people who run them. If nothing else, they are interested to know whom they'll be working with.

That's probably why bios are traffic areas on a startup website. In a simple, straightforward way, customers want to know about the people in a startup because it gives them some insight into things like quality and competence. On a more emotional level, it makes it easier for them to connect with, and give their trust to, a business they might not know much about.

As with the rest of an About page, staff bios can be simple, but shouldn't be overly dry. While a few details on education and professional background are warranted, website visitors will pay as much attention to personal trivia (like a favorite hobby or sports team) as they will actual credentials.

Photos can be used to establish impressions and convey warmth, so it's worth hiring a photographer to take quality pictures of your team and facility. That small expense of time and money can go a long way toward giving customers a sense that you are the kind of people they want to be doing business with.

Make The Most Of Your Secret Weapon

You won't see a lot of businesses following these tips, simply because they don't realize the importance of an About page on a startup website. Or if they do, they make the mistake of trying to mimic Fortune 500 firms in an effort to make a company appear larger than it actually is.

The kind of people who don't want to do business with a startup probably aren't going to buy from you anyway. And for everyone else, an About page that tells a story and has a few interesting personal tidbits is going to be far more intriguing than even the most well-written piece of standard marketing copy.

Make the most of your secret weapon by adding a little bit of spice and interest to your website's About page. Later, when you study your web analytics, you might be amazed to see how customers have responded.

9 | Mind the Details: Testing, Hosting, And Online Security

When it comes to launching a new web-based startup, lots of entrepreneurs want to focus on the parts of their business they know and understand while leaving the details to their web design team. This has to do with constraints of time and attention, obviously, but also the fact that many business people just don't understand the technical side of putting a website online.

That's certainly understandable, and a good web design partner will do their best to make sure all the minor issues get handled so that you can focus on the big picture. However, there are three areas of your web design and development project you'll want to pay at least a bit of attention to. These three details are testing, hosting, and online security.

Don't worry – I'm not going to advise you to become an expert in any of these areas. I'm simply going to suggest you make a point of knowing what needs to happen and making sure the right steps are taken. Let's tackle each of these detail areas one at a time…

Website Testing Ensures Quality

Before your website ever goes online, it's important that it be thoroughly tested to ensure that it's stable, fast-loading, and compatible with all major browsers and platforms (including web-ready smartphones and tablets). Ideally, this should all take place behind the scenes as your website is developed.

So why mention it at all? One reason is to ensure that you're working with the kind of web design company that's going to rigorously test your pages, along with any custom programming, well before your site goes live. A good creative team will bring this up with you early on, and will factor it into their release schedule.

Another reason to explicitly mention testing is because you should know how important it is and not be tempted to rush the process. Occasionally, an entrepreneur will see a web design they love, feel anxious about bringing their idea to the public, and encourage their creative team to skip testing. Or, they'll ask if the process can be sped up because they want to save on billable hours.

These are bad ideas, because startups don't get a lot of chances to impress new customers. If your website crashes, or shows flaws with security, you'll have a hard time winning back the trust of potential buyers. It's more likely that they'll decide your website isn't worth the time and never return again.

Web Hosting Puts Your Startup In The Right Neighborhood

Your web domain is the online address for your startup, but web hosting is the neighborhood and virtual land that it's built upon. Although most entrepreneurs don't really appreciate the value of great web hosting, the hosting company and plan you select could have very big consequences.

At the most basic level, your hosting dictates what kind of computer your website will be stored on, where that computer is located, and what else can be saved on its servers. Better computers, and stronger connections, mean more speed and reliability. So if you want your website to load quickly, and for customers to be able to find you on the web at all hours, it's important to choose the right hosting plan.

Additionally, premium hosting will include features that assist with online security and automatic backups. It goes without saying that you want your web-based startup to be as secure as possible, given the time, energy, and money you're putting into making it a success.

Another thing to consider is that bargain-basement hosting servers are usually shared between dozens (and sometimes hundreds) of different websites. If you have virtual "neighbors" who are engaged in questionable activities, it's possible that search engines and email providers will block those servers, meaning you could be blacklisted right along with everyone else, even though you haven't done anything wrong.

The great thing about web hosting is that a very small upgrade, in terms of cost, can bring lots of advantages. So, while web hosting might not be at the forefront of your mind very often, know that it's worth spending just a little more to make sure your business is located in the right neighborhood, where it's safe, secure, and easy to find.

Online Security Isn't Always Complicated

When entrepreneurs think of cyber security, they often picture hackers from the movies, using dozens of high-powered computers to pull off sophisticated, multimillion-dollar heists. Those kinds of online thefts probably do occur, but they are unusual. What happens far more often is thieves taking advantage of readily available information and exploiting it to get what they want.

For instance, we have all heard the advice to set complicated passwords that include uppercase and lowercase letters, numbers, and even special characters. Despite that, a lot of business people aren't aware of just how big the difference between a simple password and a complicated one can be. Automated software can crack a simple word or phrase within fractions of a second. Add in those random characters and complicated strings, however, and the same process would take years.

In the same way, updating your hosting software when prompted has the same kind of effect as setting hard-to-break passwords. Often, cyber criminals break into websites by targeting outdated WordPress websites, for example, while using known exploits. They essentially walk in through an open door or window.

The point to be made here is that even though some aspects of online security and encryption are complicated, there are simple things you can do – like setting tough passwords and keeping them to yourself, making sure your website is always updated, and taking advantage of continual backups – that make it far less likely that your startup website will be targeted by thieves, or that they'll be successful in stealing from you.

Don't Overlook The Details Of Your Web-Based Startup

There's a good chance your web design team will handle the important details related to testing, hosting, and online security for you. And they'll probably give you good advice on these topics when you need it.

Don't overlook them completely, however, or just assume they are being taken care of. Each of them is too important to leave to chance.

10 | The Successful Startup
Website Launch

The launch of your new web-based startup is a very big deal. It will probably be a moment you've looked forward to for some time, and could mark the beginning of a new chapter in your life and career.

From a technical standpoint, there isn't much to it. Your website will be designed, developed, and tested on some sort of private testing server provided by your web design company. Then, when everything is ready and fully approved, it is simply uploaded like any other set of files to your live new web-hosting server. Then your creative team can adjust a few DNS or server settings, and that's it – your web-based startup is a real company with a working website!

To make that launch as successful as possible, and smooth out any early hiccups, there are a few things you should know and pay attention to...

Make Time For One Last Test

Testing your website for technical issues is important. If you have the time, however, it's a good idea to find a few beta users who can run through its pages, as well.

During the process of designing and developing your startup website, your creative team will put it on what's called a "test" or "developing" server. This simply means that it will be stored in a place where it can look and act like any other website, but isn't actually on the Internet being promoted.

Once everyone agrees that it's finished – or at least ready for an initial test run with the public – you could have friends, colleagues, and even current customers (if you have any already) visit this test site from their own computers and pretend to interact with it. In this way, you can get some good constructive feedback. And you may stumble upon any glitches or usability issues that would have come up later.

Launching Your Startup Is All About Promotion

People love things that are brand new, which is why you might not ever get an easier chance to promote your new company than you will during its first few hours and days. If possible, you'll want to set up advertisements, email blasts, press releases, and any offline promotions well in advance of your actual launch date.

Don't let the excitement of your launch date come and go without any fanfare. Consider offering special pricing, and promote those early sales on search, social media, and advertising through any relevant industry websites. The first orders or inquiries you get don't necessarily have to be profitable. The idea is to get your best potential customers familiar with your website so they'll return again later (not to mention refer you to their friends and colleagues).

Consider Some Sort Of Giveaway

Revenue is great, but for a brand-new startup with no customers, marketing platform, or brand recognition, attention can be almost as valuable as actual currency. One way to get attention is by offering something for free. This is a tactic that has been used by some e-commerce retailers in the past, and may be an option for your startup.

To be sure, giving stuff away is a risky strategy. It can cost your new business money, and sometimes attracts people who simply want a free sample even though they wouldn't really consider buying anything from you later.

Still, having something low-cost that you can offer for nothing – if it supports your business model – can help you attract attention from the press, build a list in a hurry, and give buyers a no-obligation taste of what your new website can do.

Keep A Close Eye On Web Performance

Once your website goes live, you might be tempted to throw a party, or at least take the day off and celebrate. You'll undoubtedly have earned a break, but I advise you to stick around and pay close attention to your web analytics.

The reason is pretty simple: Customers can be unpredictable. No matter how carefully you've studied your market, implemented your promotion plan, and tested your website, there is always the chance actual visitors and customers will behave in ways you don't expect. They may respond to offers in a way you didn't expect, cause errors or misunderstandings in a surprising fashion, or even wreck your bandwidth and inventory with too many orders!

In all likelihood, you'll be very pleased at what's going on with your website after it has been launched. If you're like most of the entrepreneurs we've worked with, you'll be thrilled watching your web statistics, seeing numerous inquiries or online orders flow in. But it's best to be prepared for anything, and to see if you can spot any early trends or issues that affect your web-based startup from the outset.

Your Web-Based Startup Date Is A Special Occasion

You'll always remember what it was like to see your startup finally go live. It's a huge accomplishment for you, and a landmark occasion for your brand-new business.

Do what you can to think outside the box and promote the launch of your new company as something that's special and unique. Whether you're using giveaways, social ads, email blasts, or plain old word-of-mouth advertising, take advantage of the fact that people like things that are new and exciting. Give them something to talk about, online and off, so more and more people are being driven to your pages.

Most of all, don't forget to enjoy the fact that you've done something that nearly everyone talks about, but very few would-be entrepreneurs ever follow through with. You have taken a chance and created a new company out of nothing. That's special.

Now, it's time to see how you can market your website to start bringing new customers to your virtual front door.

11 | 3 Pieces Of Information That Make Startup Marketing "Go"

In some ways, marketing your startup business effectively is just as important as providing a product or service that resonates with your customers. It doesn't matter how good you are at anything, or how great your prices are, if no one ever hears about your company or website.

There is a lot to be written and taught about marketing for startups, and I have a lot to say on the subject. Before you worry about the specifics, though, you should remember that promoting a new business really comes down to three different things: knowing your audience, understanding who you are in the market, and building a plan for sustainable success.

Once you have those elements in place, everything else comes down to filling in the blanks. Conversely, your execution of things like search engine optimization, social media marketing, and email newsletters will never matter if you aren't working from the right kind of information.

With that in mind, let's touch on these three important cornerstones of a good startup marketing plan...

Knowing Your Customers

Who will buy from your business, and why? This is a relatively straightforward question, but one that entrepreneurs would do well to focus a lot of attention on.

That's because most markets are smaller and less open than they initially seem. While the Internet has given businesses the chance to reach everyone, it has also given customers numerous choices, with each new option being only a mouse click away. So even though anyone who buys the product or service you sell could be a potential prospect, the reality is your pool of buyers is probably much more narrow.

Suppose for a moment you sold a kind of handmade specialty soda directly from your website. Theoretically, anyone who was feeling thirsty might be a good potential customer. However, those who have a preference for all-natural drinks might be a subgroup. Also, you could find that only a small segment of the population can afford your gourmet sodas, and would be willing to wait for them to be delivered to their home. Additionally, others might decide to take their business elsewhere because of language barriers, delivery times, or other constraints.

This is just a simple and fictional example, but it illustrates an important idea. Your real market is often much smaller than the one you could easily imagine.

That's not necessarily bad news, however. Even though you could be selling your products or services to fewer people than you think, that also means you're free to tighten your campaigns and devote your time and energy to the people who are willing to buy from you initially, place the largest orders, and come back to you again and again. Narrowing down to that group means less wasted time and money, and gives you a bigger return on all of your campaigns.

Get to know your best possible customers. Understand who they are, in terms of demographics, and what moves them to action when they make buying decisions.

Finding Your Place In The Market

It's not just about knowing who your best customers are, but also knowing what your business represents to them. In other words, you have to find the key differentiators that separate you from your closest competitors – remembering, of course, that your "closest" competitor might be far in real life, but next door online.

Without the knowledge of why someone would buy from you instead of another business, you really don't have the basis for a successful marketing campaign. Luckily, there are literally dozens of good answers to that question.

Perhaps customers will buy from you because you charge less than anyone else. Or, your products and/or service might be superior. It could be that you can get their purchases to them faster, or serve a niche that no one else focuses on. Things like geography and marketing personality could also come into play.

When you understand who your buyers are, and what your business means to them, it shapes your marketing in an important way. It helps you find not only the right messages to put forth, but the perfect tone or personality for your company. You aren't just offering a product or service and looking for buyers; instead, you're trying to make the right match between what you can do and what others actually want or need.

If you never find a differentiator, then you can't give customers a compelling reason to spend their money with your startup instead of an established company they already know. Do what it takes to research the market, interview buyers, or brainstorm the answers you need.

Bridging The Gap Between Your Startup And The Market

Once you know what your business is about, and who it's really for, there's only one thing that's missing: your plan for informing customers about what you have to offer.

There are lots of ways to do this, and you'll probably want to try several. What matters at this point isn't the specific tactics you'll put into play, but that you choose ones that make sense for your budget and audience, and that they work together cohesively.

For instance, if a consultation with your web design team shows that customers look for your type of product or service on search engines, then you'll undoubtedly want to focus a lot of attention on promoting your website via Google. At the same time, if sponsored search ads are incredibly expensive, then you might focus on organic search engine optimization through long key phrases.

What matters here is that you can bring your plan, message, and resources together in a way that makes sense. It's very common for entrepreneurs to want to try everything, or experiment with flashy tactics they've read about. If these activities don't fit into the bigger context of what you're trying to accomplish, however – or what you can actually spend time or money on – they can turn out to be costly distractions.

Preparation Is The Key To Startup Marketing Success

Entrepreneurs can be energetic and impetuous people, and those wonderful qualities drive them to take risks and action when others would wait. At the same time, those same women and men need to realize how important preparation is to the process of marketing a web-based startup.

When your business is just getting off the ground, you don't have time or resources to waste. Make sure you have a deep understanding of the three key pieces of information you'll need for your marketing campaigns before you get started promoting your website in earnest.

12 | Get Your Startup Branding Right From Day One

For a lot of entrepreneurs, getting a business up and running, and profitable, is the first order of business. That means designing a website and then putting together the accompanying marketing materials on the fly with little thought for long-term messaging and branding.

That's certainly understandable, but it's short-sighted. That's because your brand identity – regardless of whether you build it intentionally or not – is going to stick with your startup for a long time. The choices you make in the beginning can come back to reward or haunt you for years to come.

The great thing about branding for web-based startups is that your company's identity can be whatever you want it to be. You aren't constrained in any way by history, tradition, or even familiarity. It's up to you to decide what your marketing should look and feel like.

Let's take a closer peek at a few of the ways you can make your startup branding both consistent and extraordinary...

Pay Close Attention To The Design Of Branding Elements

That marketing personality I referred to is essentially your brand concept. The way it's translated into real-life communications is through the different elements of your brand. These are the "ingredients" that make your brand recognizable.

You could realistically come up with a list of hundreds of branding elements, but the most noticeable and important are your logo, colors, fonts, and communication style. These are the elements that will carry over from one piece or campaign to the next. And just as importantly, changing them later on will mean wholesale modifications throughout your website, advertisements, and marketing documents.

The point I'm trying to make here is that you should pay very close attention to the designs and early decisions that are made about your brand. You'll be stuck with things like logos and color schemes later on, so make sure that you like what you choose, and that it represents your vision for what you want your business to become.

Know What Your Startup's Brand Identity Is

Building a new brand for a new company can be quite the challenge. In fact, a lot of brands are created almost by accident, as entrepreneurs and their designers make seemingly small decisions that add up to bigger patterns and impressions.

Sometimes that leads to a happy accident; more often than not, however, it's a prescription for headaches. The better course of action is to know what your web-based startup's brand is right off the bat. Make conscious decisions about each of the elements (which we'll get to in a second), as well as have an idea of what you want the public-facing personality of your business to be like.

People like brands because they form an instant expectation. The obvious example here is a business like McDonald's. Regardless of how you feel about the fast food giant, there's one thing you can be sure of: When you walk into one of their restaurants, you know *exactly* what you're going to get.

Even if you are aiming for a much different market than they are, it's important that your brand have the same kind of power and associations. You want customers to know what your business is all about, and what an experience with your startup is going to be like. One of the subtle ways you can reinforce those notions is by maintaining consistency from one interaction to the next.

A good way to foster consistency within your branding efforts is to create a style worksheet, which can also be known as a brand guide. This is just a document that lays out things like the spelling of key names or terms, specifications for where and how your logo should be used, and any preferences you have for grammar and tone as well as any other related elements of your overall brand that should be preserved in future activities where your brand is promoted.

This kind of stylesheet can be used internally, and with creative vendors, to ensure that your brand is consistent over time.

Think Ahead

As I've already mentioned, one of the classic mistakes entrepreneurs make, when it comes to branding, is thinking only of their needs in the moment. If things go right, your business is going to grow by leaps and bounds... so you'll want to lay the foundation for a brand that grows with it.

This is partly to help create that consistency I've referenced before. But it's also because the last thing you're going to need a few months down the road is to spend more money on design to fix things that weren't done correctly the first time. This is surprisingly common, as web-based startups take off and then find that the brand they have doesn't really fit the image they're trying to project out into the market.

Think ahead to what you want your brand to look and feel like in a few years. How do you want others to think of your company? Incorporate those notes into your initial branding efforts. They might not all matter at the moment, but they can help steer you in the right direction as your business takes shape.

Good Branding Helps You Build

While it's easy to think of your brand as a collection of colors and images, it can and should be so much more. Your brand is what customers think of when your company comes to mind, and the emotional response they have to your business.

Humans tend to act on emotion, and impression, as much as they do fact. Lots of devices can do what an iPhone can, but none of them have the same kind of sleek appeal and impressive form. There are probably dozens of places to get coffee within walking distance of your current location, but buyers flock to Starbucks because they associate it with a certain kind of experience and lifestyle.

The list could go on and on, expanding to clothing designers, beverage companies, sports teams, and many other different parts of life and business. In each case, you'll find there are powerful brands making a big impact in the market. Think ahead, and yours could be the next one.

13 | Startup Marketing Basics: Speed, Affordability, And Positive ROI

Putting a marketing plan into place for a startup company is a much different exercise than doing the same thing for an established business. For one thing, a brand-new business is a blank slate, with no name recognition or established branding. And for another, startups have different marketing goals than other businesses do. They need to establish positive cash flow quickly, and can't necessarily afford to take big risks that might not pay off.

Those are sweeping generalizations, of course, that don't necessarily apply to every startup. Some well-funded ventures have the capital to be patient and experiment. Even in those cases, however, it's almost always better to get the business moving in the right direction and have extra reserves than it is to spend months or years wondering whether the right concept is in place.

Because speed, affordability, and positive ROI are all so important to marketing for web-based startups, let's take a look at each one in slightly greater depth...

Why Speed Matters In Startup Marketing

When you are trying to get your new business off the ground, there's no time to waste. From the moment your website goes live, it's a race to ensure you can find customers and become profitable before you either run out of capital or decide that your business plan just won't fly.

It's sad, but not unusual, for new companies to run out of funding right as they seem to be making a bit of traction. This can be the result of market conditions, of course, but poor planning also plays a role. If you put all of your energy and resources into longer-term strategies like search engine optimization and social media interaction, then it's going to be an agonizing wait while the market catches up to your concept.

For most startups, it makes sense to devote some resources toward search advertising, guest posting, email marketing, and other strategies that bring results quickly. They may or may not be affordable and efficient over time, but they can help you find those priceless first few customers and start generating a bit of cash flow while you push forward with other concepts.

Startups Should Invest In Affordable Tactics

Speed and affordability don't always go hand-in-hand, but it's a balance that has to be managed. Just as startups usually don't have any time to lose, neither do they have money to waste.

Frequently, the answer is to take bigger ideas and use them in very specific ways. For example, new businesses can take advantage of pay-per-click advertising (through Google AdWords and Facebook) and use them to target long-tail search terms and highly segmented audiences. By essentially "cherry picking" the best customers for the offer, the business can spend less than it would on a larger campaign while still generating immediate results.

During the first days of your startup marketing campaigns, the analytics data you get from your website and advertising platforms can be invaluable. That's because *nothing* you invest in is affordable – no matter how low the cost – unless it's generating a positive return.

It doesn't matter if you can bring new visitors to your website for half a cent for each click if you're getting no interaction and no conversions. Keep that in mind and remember that affordability isn't just about price, but the degree to which you can generate real results.

That, of course, brings us into the related area of return on investment.

Startups Must Generate A Positive ROI

Again, it's not exactly an enormous secret to suggest that businesses need to make money from their marketing plans in order to succeed. Any accountant or entrepreneur could point that out. This plays out in two important ways when it comes to startup marketing, though: Owners should pursue strategies that have a high probability of success, and need to keep a close eye on the results of individual campaigns.

This holds true even if revenue isn't your primary concern. In some startups, just gaining market share, and a list of initial users, is the first consideration. Your business might be in a position where gaining an audience is important now, because you can monetize their activity later.

Either way, it pays to remember some marketing tactics tend to work for almost any company that puts them to good use. To go back to my earlier example, targeted PPC advertising and email newsletters are among the most proven ways to keep customers and generate revenue. At the same time, running viral social campaigns can be very hit or miss.

Startups would do well to focus most of their early marketing firepower on campaigns that are very likely to show short-term returns, even if those might not be as spectacular as the results they could achieve elsewhere. In other words, look to hit singles instead of homeruns.

Also, know that your ability to track the effectiveness of individual campaigns (one PPC ad group versus another, the results from a single email list, etc.) can help you to make smart decisions going forward. As revenue starts to come in, you want to be able to figure out where your customers are coming from and pour more resources into the ideas that are working and waste less money on those that aren't.

Make Speed, Affordability, And Positive ROI The Focus Of Your Startup Marketing
Often, entrepreneurs come to us with a vision for a web-based business, but not necessarily a plan for turning it into a reality. In other words, the inspiration you have for your startup might not include day-to-day marketing details.

If that's the case, don't make the mistake of throwing all of your time and resources into concepts that are shiny, edgy, or hot at the moment. Instead, look for the strategies that you can use to achieve results quickly, find customers without spending a fortune, and be very likely to achieve a positive rate of return.

Those should be the big priorities for your business at the start, and could be the keys for turning your entrepreneurial vision into a reality.

14 | Effective Search Marketing For Startups

For most web-based businesses, Google represents the number one source of new traffic and customers. That shouldn't be surprising, given that the world's most popular online destination currently processes more than 2 *billion* inquiries on a daily basis. You could add to that the traffic coming from other search engines, like Yahoo and Bing, that also factors into the mix to a lesser degree.

Even if you weren't familiar with the numbers, you are probably already aware search engines need to make up a big part of your marketing plan. But how do you get them to send potential customers your way?

Traditionally, there are two ways: organic search engine optimization and paid search advertising (the ads you see displayed on search engines). Both are just different ways of reaching the same audience. And so, even though there are important distinctions between each, it makes sense to discuss them together in this section.

Let's take a look at what you need to know...

Organic Search Engine Optimization Is Simpler Than You Think

There are entire books and seminars devoted to the topic of SEO, and the technical details are virtually endless. However, what you really need to know as an entrepreneur is that Google works by keeping its users happy. When someone types a phrase or question into a search engine box (or more and more frequently, speaks it into their smartphone), Google's job is to find the very best part of the Internet that matches up to that inquiry.

To do so, they use a number of different indicators, like the age of your website, the name of your domain, the content on your pages, and the number of links pointing at your website. The more content you have, and the more authoritative your website seems, the more prominently your pages will be displayed within the search engine listings.

Again, this is a simplified view of the way search engines work, and Google's algorithm is a complex mathematical beast that incorporates more than 200 different factors into search listings. But if you can remember that better websites with more content and links rise to the top, you'll know enough to stand out from your competitors.

Paid Search Marketing Works Differently

The great thing about organic SEO is that it can bring you lots of targeted web traffic at no cost. However, if you want to skip to the head of the line, test a concept, or target buyers in an additional way, paid search ads are a great alternative.

You've undoubtedly seen search engine pay-per-click (PPC) ads many times already today if you've been engaging with any search engines. Again, search advertising is a big topic, but the basics are simple: You choose keywords and phrases that your potential customers would search, write ads that they can notice and click on when they search those phrases, and then decide how much you'll pay for each visit to your website.

The better your ads perform, and the more relevant your website is, the less Google will charge you for each click to your website. PPC ads are a great way to get your business up and running, especially when you don't have an existing flow of organic traffic coming to your website already.

Both Types Of Search Marketing Rely On Precision

Whether you're going to use organic SEO, paid search ads, or both, what you really want to keep in mind is that it's all about precision in niche marketing. It's easy to be drawn in by the fact that there are lots of phrases that get big visits on the web; unfortunately, many of these are too general in nature to signify any real buying intent.

As an easy example, suppose someone searches "baseball" on Google. They could be looking for tickets to a game, statistics for their favorite player, the history of the sport, or one of any other of a dozen different things. On the other hand, someone who searches "Little League baseball jerseys in Boston" has told you quite a bit about what their intentions are.

The point to take away from this is that, in both organic SEO and paid search advertising, you want to target the people who are most likely to become customers. That means finding the intersection between phrases that generate decent search volume, don't have overwhelming competition, and suggest a certain amount of buyer knowledge and/or intent. If you can focus on those factors, you'll have the groundwork for profitable campaigns.

Consider Using Ads Before Organic SEO

Some entrepreneurs prefer to focus their attention on organic search engine optimization, rather than spend money on paid search ads, for the simple reason that organic traffic is free. However, that notion ignores two important factors.

The first is that organic SEO often requires outside assistance, especially when a particular market or industry is already full of competitors who have been optimizing their websites for years. That "free" traffic can become expensive quickly and/or takes months to return decent results. The second factor is that PPC advertising can be put into place almost instantly. So not only can it show immediate dividends, but the results of a paid campaign can be used to steer organic search in the right direction.

Few things are as painful as setting up an extensive search engine optimization effort over the course of months, only to find that the phrases you're targeting aren't generating the kind of traffic or conversions you had hoped for. With a small budget and a few weeks, you can often find the answers to these types of questions in advance.

Good PPC Advertising Is All About Constraints

Even though it doesn't take a lot of time to set up search advertising, you don't want to rush. That's because every click you bring to your website is going to cost you money, so you certainly want to keep the right constraints in place to avoid paying money on visits that aren't likely to result in sales.

For example, putting constraints into place for things like language, location, and time of day are good for keeping away from searchers who wouldn't really be a good fit for what you offer. In addition, you can add negative keywords to your account that stop your ads from being triggered when searchers use certain terms (like "free" or the name of a competitor).

The more constraints you have on your search marketing accounts, the lower the odds are that you'll burn through your budget without having your ad shown to real buyers. That's online advertising efficiency at its best.

Any Good Search Campaign Is Optimized Twice

Business owners will often talk about optimizing their websites, or their ads. Usually, what they are referring to is the process of tweaking headings, links, and keywords to ensure that they can draw in as much targeted traffic as possible.

That's undoubtedly important, but don't forget that another type of optimization is needed – you must optimize your website for conversions. In other words, bringing visitors to your pages is fantastic, but it means nothing if you can't turn them into customers, or at least leads.

With that in mind, you should keep a close eye on your web analytics so you can know what visitors are doing and responding to at all times. And it means you should try to convince customers to connect with you on social media websites, or sign up for your email newsletter, if they don't decide to do business with you right away.

By staying in contact with a searcher, you make it possible to follow up with them later and increase the odds that someone who didn't know you before will eventually become a customer. This type of optimization can be even more important than the initial setup needed to bring visitors to your website in the first place.

Search engine marketing is all about meeting customers and generating conversions… just like everything else you do to promote your new web-based business. If you can keep these tips in mind, you'll be able to avoid the common trap of focusing too tightly on the technical details and missing the forest for the trees.

15 | Startups And Social Media

Like search engine marketing, social media is a huge (and growing) topic that can't really be conquered in one article or book chapter. And yet, the principles are simple enough that you can learn them, use them, and give yourself an enormous advantage over the other businesses competing for attention in your space – regardless of whether they are startups or established companies.

Lots of entrepreneurs gravitate toward social media for a couple of reasons: Sites like Facebook and Twitter are generally free to use, and most people who are starting a web-based company are already familiar with them. Plus, a good social campaign can easily bring you thousands of visits every week.

Using social media to promote your startup business is different than posting quick thoughts or family photos for friends to see, however. So, let's take a closer look at what you need to know and do to promote your website and social network...

Set Up Profiles On All The Major Social Platforms

In order to make social media work for your startup, of course, you have to have a presence on all the major social platforms. That means setting up profiles and pages, separate from your personal accounts, on Facebook, Twitter, Google+, YouTube, Instagram, LinkedIn, and any others that you think are relevant to your company or industry.

Take the time to set up complete profiles on each of these sites (not just your favorites), taking extra care to use high-quality photographs and accurate contact information. You want to make it as simple as possible for potential customers to find you on social sites, figure out what you do, and know where they should go to take the next step if they're interested.

Know Where (And When) Your Customers Hang Out

Even though you should have complete profiles on all the major social media platforms, you won't necessarily give them all equal time and attention. But, you shouldn't necessarily direct your efforts toward the ones that you personally like to use, but the social websites that your customers prefer.

Usually, the men and women in a particular market will tend to cluster around one or two different social media platforms. For instance, at the time of this writing, college students can often be found on Twitter and YouTube. Baby boomers, conversely, prefer Facebook and LinkedIn. The more you know about what your buyers prefer, the easier it is for you to post messages in places where they'll come across them.

Don't forget that timing matters as well. Just as different demographics gravitate to different social destinations, there can also be better or worse times of the day and week to post. Make it easy to get noticed by posting when the majority of your market is likely to be online and paying attention.

Balance Information And Marketing Content With Entertainment

Posting information, ideas, and photos to your social accounts is easy. Getting potential customers to pay attention might not be.

To make an impact, you have to be careful about the way you present yourself on these websites. That's because most people log in to social media pages to have fun and connect with friends (with LinkedIn being the obvious exception, since it's based on networking). So if what they read from you seems like a blatant promotion or advertisement, they may just ignore it.

At the same time, you can't do your startup much good by posting nothing but cat pictures and inspirational quotes. So try to balance the fine line between entertainment and information. Create content that invites views and shares, but also lead it back to your industry and insert links to your website. If you can manage to grab interest while keeping the focus on your company, your social media campaigns will be effective.

Post Things That Are Easy To Pass On

Another thing to love about social media marketing is that it can be used to expand your audience quickly. That is, if you post something online and your fans, friends, and followers share it, your content can end up being seen by a much wider audience than you would expect.

The key to making this happen is posting things that are easy to share. Photos with captions, for example, are perfect for your followers to click and distribute to their own groups. So are short statistics, sayings, and ideas.

There's nothing wrong with producing longer articles and white papers, but these should be saved for your website, blog, and email campaigns, which can also be teased on your social channels linking back to your blog. To make the most of your social profiles, post content that is quick, snappy, and to the point – that's what others will pass on for you.

Have A Point To Your Social Activity

I alluded to this already, but it's worth pointing out in greater depth: Your social media marketing campaigns shouldn't feel like a personal feed. Although you can certainly get attention, and even interaction, by ranting about your favorite news, sports, or political stories, that's not going to do anything to help your startup grow. In fact, it's likely to turn off big segments of the market and make you look like an amateur.

Remember that, and always tie the social posting that comes from your startup's accounts back to your business or industry. Don't be afraid to let your hair down once in a while, or let buyers get a peek behind the curtain; when you do, however, use it to show the personal side of your company and present yourself as the kind of entrepreneur people want to root for.

If there's no point to your social activity, other than your personal passions and pet peeves, your campaigns aren't going to generate any traction. When that happens, you're just wasting time and energy that could be put to better uses elsewhere.

Becoming A Social Superstar
Takes Practice and Patience

While there certainly have been startup companies that have been able to build up an enormous social media following overnight, the reality is that it usually takes a bit of time to find fans, hone your message, and develop a consistent flow of traffic from social platforms toward your website.

Be consistent with your posting, and with the type of ideas you put out into the world, and you'll start to see results. In some businesses, social media is becoming even more important than search engines. Follow the guidelines I have given you, and you'll be primed to make the most of both.

16 | Local Online Marketing For Startups

One of the great things about starting an online company is that you can reach customers anywhere in the world, so long as the buyers you're looking for have an Internet connection. And yet, there are some very good reasons you might want to focus on local customers, at least during the weeks and months while your web-based startup is getting off the ground.

Let's look at why local customers are so important, and what you can do to find them…

Why Local Customers Matter To New Companies

Given that your pool of customers on the web is essentially infinite, why bother specifically targeting local customers at all?

One reason has to do with cost. By restricting the size of your campaigns to those who are closest to you geographically, you can fund online ads without spending a fortune. That's particularly true if you're trying to launch an MVP version of your website. Additionally, buyers in your area are likely to be the ones that you know and understand best, so your message is likely to resonate with them and generate an immediate response.

Trust is another factor. Customers find it easier to believe in businesses, and individual people, who are close by and similar to themselves. So when you're trying to establish a business with no existing brand or name recognition, you might find customers who live down the road are among the easiest to win... even when you're doing business online.

Basic Local SEO Is Easy

Another reason to pay attention to local buyers is because Google, Facebook, and other online hubs of activity make it easy for you to reach them. By adding simple geographic keywords to your website (for instance, "Boston web design," or "Boston web development"), you give searchers strong clues as to where you are located.

Google, as well as other search engines and social portals, will notice this and direct people from the same general area in your direction. This is known as local search engine optimization, but it works in many different ways on the web. People prefer to do business with others who are geographically close, all things considered, so make the most of it and bring those local buyers to your website.

This is partly because of the algorithmic preferences I've already mentioned. Google will reward you with higher quality scores if you're advertising to buyers in your area. It's also because you can use keywords, headlines, and other phrases that will appeal to customers who are nearby, boosting the response rates of your campaigns.

And of course, as I've already mentioned, restricting the scope of your PPC and Internet advertising means a smaller number of impressions and a lower overall budget. That can be important for startups that are trying to maximize every dollar spent.

Use The Power Of The Press

One underrated tool that not enough entrepreneurs take advantage of is the local press. Starting a company is an exciting thing; it happens around the world every day, but probably not nearly as often in your own neighborhood.

For that reason, editors, business journal reporters, and bloggers who are close by might be interested to know about your company, and your reasons for starting it. In fact, they might even have personal ties to your business, or see it as being newsworthy for others in the area.

Keep Your Advertising Localized

The bigger your online advertising campaigns get, the harder they are to manage... and the more potential there is for waste in your budget. The opposite is also true: The more you focus on finding local customers through the Internet, the less you have to spend to generate conversions.

Make sure your press releases are being sent to outlets in your geographic area, and emphasize your location within your posts and communication. You may just find the local press has a strong interest in what you're doing, and can help spread the word about your company on your behalf.

Encourage Positive Word-Of-Mouth

For all the great ways there are to promote your company online, few sales tactics are nearly as effective as old-fashioned word-of-mouth. When you can get people speaking to each other about your products or services, you greatly increase the odds that new buyers are going to find their way to your startup.

Although this isn't as true as it once was, people tend to know each other within specific cities and neighborhoods. So word-of-mouth advertising often spreads geographically, even in the digital age.

You should do everything you can to encourage people to say good things about your startup online. And then, you can make sure other customers in the area see this, both by using local marketing and by signing up for geographic directories. That way, buyers can find them and take notice.

Local Can Mean Different Things To Different Startups

As important as I think local marketing and promotion is, it's important to note that the term can mean different things to different entrepreneurs. For example, if you live in a very large metropolitan area, local might mean the city, or even just your neighborhood within it. In another place without so many residents (and competitors), "local" might mean your state or province.

And sometimes what's "close by" doesn't really have much to do with geography at all, but the type of customer you want to attract. For instance, if your web-based startup is directed at dentists who do advanced cosmetic work, they might represent a small community that's spread throughout North America.

That's not really the definition of "local," of course, but the same principles I've given you here would still apply. What matters isn't necessarily the address you would put on an envelope, but where your most obvious source of initial customers lives, works, and hangs out. Identify them as your local market, and then take steps to dominate it.

Build Upon Your Local Success

Finding local customers can be a great way to get your startup established, bring in some early revenue, and start generating some positive word-of-mouth. Plus, you can target local buyers relatively inexpensively, and use what you learn from the experience to expand your campaigns to a nationwide – or even international – audience.

If you're looking for the easiest way to test the concept, create revenues, and prove that your concept can work in the market, strongly consider targeting local customers first.

17 | Common Mistakes In Web-Based Startups

Unfortunately, there are as many ways to ruin a new business as there are to make it succeed. Even worse, you can take a perfectly viable and innovative concept and watch it fail if you don't know the major errors to look out for.

For all the joy it gives me to watch a new company take off and fly, it breaks my heart to see an entrepreneur put his or her heart and soul into a dream that never really gets off the ground. I like to remind clients that websites often die from preventable illnesses. That is, there are lots of avoidable mistakes that are surprisingly easy to make.

Here are seven of the most prominent you should look out for. Beware of them at every stage, beginning with the moment when you first decide to turn your startup into an actual company, and continuing for every year you remain in business...

#1: Ignoring Problems With The Concept

Let's face it: Not every idea for a business is a winner. Sometimes the market is too small, or saturated. Other times, the concept just isn't innovative enough, or conversely, is so far outside the box that it doesn't make sense to your average buyer.

As an experienced web developer and entrepreneur myself, I always make a point of letting a client know if I think they have problems with their web concept. Note, however, that some vendors aren't quite as ethical, and might take your money even if they don't think you'll succeed.

The point here is that you should think your business idea through as carefully as possible, and seek out expert advice wherever you can find it. There's not really a "sure thing" in the world of web-based startups, but you want to do whatever you can to put the odds on your side.

#2: Forgetting To Study The Competition

When you're trying to launch a brand-new company, it helps to know what has and hasn't worked for others. And yet, many entrepreneurs behind web-based startups don't take much time to study the competition.

Sometimes, they'll tell you it's because "we don't have any competitors yet." That's rarely true. You might not have another company that's trying to do what you do exactly how you want to do it, but there are likely other established businesses in your industry (Amazon had Barnes & Noble to contend with in the beginning, for example). And if you truly *don't* have any competitors, that can be a problem because it could signal a market that's too small.

You aren't looking to copy your competitors, of course, just to know who they are, where they're at, and which ideas or business models have been successful for them. And you want to know what will make your startup different, and the ways you can explain that to potential customers.

#3: Not Monetizing Your Idea Correctly

You can't build a business without knowing where revenue is going to come from. Are you going to get money from subscribers, sell directly to customers, or work on an advertising platform?

Never make assumptions here. If possible, look for other businesses that are following a model similar to yours (as I just advised), or at least conduct a few tests and/or interviews to make sure that what you're offering has value to the people you are expecting to pay for it.

If you can't monetize your business model – or if you monetize it in a way that doesn't make sense or isn't sustainable – then it's only a matter of time before your startup is a memory.

#4: Prioritizing Web Design Fees Or Aesthetics Over Web Functionality

Business owners *love* looking at new web designs. There's just something about a fresh mockup that's exciting, especially when it means your vision is coming to life. Pay too much attention to the aesthetics, though, and you'll overlook issues of functionality and marketing. The end result is a website that looks great but does nothing or can't be found online.

A similar mistake is often made when entrepreneurs stare at competing bids and choose the one with the lowest up-front cost instead of the vendor who offers the most value in terms of ROI later. It's nice to save money, but what does it matter if your startup is never profitable?

You might have noticed that the bulk of this book has been about web development, innovation, and spreading the word on your company. That's intentional. These are the factors that will make you successful. Don't miss the forest for the trees, and put so much attention on aesthetics or prices that you end up with a website that can't help you accomplish your actual business goals.

#5: Failing To Put A Marketing Plan In Place

In a web-based startup, your website and Internet marketing plan *are* the business keys, so don't shortchange your future success by trying to save a few dollars here and there. It just isn't worth it.

Your marketing plan isn't something you want to develop on the fly, after your website has gone live. Instead, you should have a promotional plan that accompanies your MVP, a regular schedule of reviews and analytic checks to ensure you're on the right track, and a set of concepts you can use to start expanding once your business takes off.

Without the right marketing plan, you can be sure your company won't ever go anywhere. Pay close attention to this part of the process.

#6: *Trying To Do Too Much At Once*

There is a flip side to what I just wrote in the previous note. When you're thinking too big, trying to do too much at once, and attempting to make your startup "everything to everyone," everything suffers.

Remember: The reason I encourage you to develop an MVP version of your website wasn't just to save on time and money, but also to give you the space to test your concept. That's twice as important with your marketing plan, since you'll be attempting to share your vision of the business with the world. Try to do it all, and you might end up accomplishing nothing.

I advised you earlier to begin your marketing with ideas that you can expect to be successful and show a sustainable positive rate of return early.

Why not start with those ideas and work it out from there? Focus your attention (and budget) on those kinds of concepts, and you'll avoid the common trap of attempting to bite off more than you can chew.

#7: *Not Keeping One Eye On The Bottom Line*

Most new businesses have to keep a close eye on the budget. If you are launching your web-based startup from your own savings, or financing from the bank, the risk of running out of cash when you need it most is very real. And even if you have a large credit line or substantial investment, showing the wrong kinds of returns early on could dampen enthusiasm for your project and cause those funds to disappear.

One of your first missions as an entrepreneur is to show (either yourself, or the world) that your concept can be translated into a profitable website. Never get so excited about developing new ideas, planning marketing campaigns, or doing anything else that you let the financial side of things get out of hand. Make that mistake, and your startup dream could be over very quickly.

I can guarantee you that right now, as you read this, some entrepreneur with a great idea for a web-based business is struggling with one of these issues, and it's going to strangle their new company (along with the time and money they sank into creating it). Be on the lookout, and ensure that your startup isn't the next one to disappear because of a problem you could have seen coming.

18 | Building A Great Reputation For Your Startup

By definition, a new company doesn't really have a reputation to worry about. In customers' minds, your business is a blank slate. There are good and bad aspects to that, but you should know that establishing and building a great reputation needs to be one of your most important goals.

What is your company's reputation? It's simply the sum of what people say or feel about the business and brand. It's online reviews of your products and services, news stories about your company, and even the way people feel about you – the company's founder – as an individual.

All of these feelings and impressions add up. And when they do, they can make it far more or less likely that someone will visit your website for the first time, and whether they'll return in the future.

Knowing that, let's look at how you can build a great reputation for your startup...

Know What Your Startup Is About

At several points, I've challenged you to think carefully about what your web concept really is, and why a customer would decide to do business with you instead of a competitor. Remember, some of the buyers you need to make your startup fly are currently working with another company. Why would they switch to you?

When you know the answers to those questions, building the right kind of reputation gets a lot easier. That's because you know what your relative strengths are, and which segment of the market you are targeting. The more you know about your startup and understand the relative value you can provide with your concept, the easier it is to build the right kind of reputation with the correct audience for your products or services.

Take Every Piece Of Feedback Seriously

One thing first-time business owners struggle to understand is that every piece of feedback – and especially feedback that's given in public, or online – needs to be taken seriously. Even if you don't think someone's issue or concern is poignant enough to warrant consideration, you can bet that other potential customers will.

Besides that, it is an often-stated notion that for every one person who takes the time to tell you about a problem, there are nine others who are thinking it and have said nothing. So, if someone calls or emails your company, or takes the time to point out something they didn't like, pay attention. Figure out whether it's an isolated incident, or an issue that needs to be corrected before the rest of your business can be harmed.

Likewise, if you get good news from a customer, look for ways you can emphasize their positive feedback in what you do going forward. This is a big way of saying that you should learn from both your successes and your failures. That might not be a new sentiment, but it's one that can save your business and its reputation.

One final thought here is to never let a bad review fester. If someone has a negative experience with your company, do what you can to make it right immediately. If you brush off the encounter, they may post something online that poisons opinion against you for hundreds of potential buyers, or more. No business can afford to have lots of negative feedback floating around on the Internet, especially not a new one.

Find Fans And Encourage Them
To Spread The Word

New businesses need customers, but even more than that they need *fans*. In this case, I'm not talking about individuals who will click a thumbs up button on your Facebook page, but men and women who are truly passionate about your startup and will help spread the word.

There are a few different ways to find these fans. One is by using marketing that appeals directly to them, their concerns, and even their sense of humor. You can also provide excellent service, and be diligent with posting to your social profiles. Another way is to tell your story in a way that makes buyers root for you.

Once you have these fans, let them know how valuable they are to you and encourage them to spread the word through email, social media, and other means. You might even want to consider giving discounts or bonuses for certain types of referrals. Your fans can spread the right kind of reputation much faster than your online marketing campaigns ever could, and with a lot more credibility.

Manage Your Own Reputation, As Well

Although you as a person are technically and reasonably very much different from your business, you should always remember some customers will have trouble making the distinction. And, as the founder and public face of your startup, you'll be tied to your venture in customers' minds forever.

This is worth mentioning here because if your reputation takes a hit, then it's very likely the reputation of your startup will be damaged, as well. We've all seen what happens when well-known business people and media personalities end up in the news for the wrong reasons. The exact same thing can happen to you, on a smaller scale, if you come to be associated with the wrong kinds of opinions or troubles.

I'm certainly not advising you to live your life in a way that keeps you from ever having a disagreement or a unique point of view. What I am telling you, though, is that being publicly associated with anything that's controversial or unpopular can affect your ability to grow and establish your company. Become known for the right things, and you'll have an easier time making your business a successful one.

Always Look For Ways To Get Better

Great reputations are the natural result of great businesses. When your company is doing the right things, and providing value again and again, people are going to talk about it. So, if you're always looking for ways to get better, you can be sure your reputation will continually be improving.

Impressions matter, especially when you're trying to convince customers to take a chance on a company they haven't heard of or worked with before. Never forget that, and use the advice I've given you here to establish and grow a reputation that makes it easy for buyers to trust you.

19 | How Startups Can Use Web Analytics Intelligently

No matter how well planned and thought out the concept for your web-based startup is, there are bound to be some surprises along the way. Campaigns and ideas you were *sure* would be successful will flounder. Some products or services that you expected to be the building blocks of your bottom line may fall flat, while others that were quick inspirations will exceed every hope you had for them.

The point I'm driving at is that success in online entrepreneurship is all about studying what's happening around you and then making the right adjustments. That starts with your web analytics.

Many business people who aren't intimately familiar with web design fear the graphs and statistics displayed by analytics packages. They feel overwhelmed by the information that's on display, and may ignore them altogether. That's a mistake. By getting to know a few important metrics, you can see what's happening on your website. Even better, you can infer what customers like, want, and are responding to.

Here are a few tips you can use to make the most of your web analytics package and see your online business grow in leaps and bounds...

Know Your Traffic Sources

The traffic sources reports offered by your web analytics package give you arguably the most important piece of information you'll find about your online activity. That's because, when you know where your customers are coming from, you get a couple of key insights. The first is which marketing ideas or campaigns are working for you; and the second has to do with the mindset of your potential customers.

When you know what your traffic sources are, and can trace them back to earlier efforts (such as email, organic search engine optimization, PPC campaigns, etc.), devoting your resources to the right channels becomes a lot simpler. You can back the "winners" in your campaigns and de-emphasize the tools that haven't shown promise.

More importantly, however, you can know what your potential customers are likely to be looking for just by seeing what brought them to your website in the first place. If you can understand their questions, challenges, or frame of mind, you can give them exactly what they need.

Look For Activity And Engagement

Studying web analytics isn't just about knowing where your customers are coming from, of course. You also want to know what's happening once visitors arrive at your website. Which pages are they spending time on? Where are they coming into your site, and when are they leaving? Are they converting into sales or leads?

Through the activity and engagement on your website, you can discover which topics are most interesting to your customers, and what kinds of messages they respond to. That can help you shape and tweak your content, but it can also show you where there are areas for growth.

Remember: No website is perfect, especially when it has first been launched. But, by studying analytics and customer behavior, you can take a good concept and mold it to be an ideal fit for the market you are targeting.

Take Away Roadblocks

Just as a close look at your web analytics can help you find the parts of your website that are popular, it can also reveal which pages, topics, or ideas could use a bit of work or revision.

Specifically, you'll probably notice that some parts of your website have high bounce rates – indicating that visitors came to those pages but left without taking any further action. These represent missed opportunities and "dead ends" that stop you from winning new business.

You can't afford to have any soft spots on your web presence. Any dead weight that prevents you from growing your business needs to be taken away and replaced with something that's more compelling to your customers. The best way to find and fix those problems is by studying your web analytics.

Spot Trends In The Market

Another good side effect of being fluent with your web analytics is that you can sometimes identify trends and opportunities before they actually take shape.

This usually occurs when you notice that visitors are coming to your website using a brand-new set of search terms. Or, that a certain post or page invites comments and feedback that go in a direction you weren't expecting. Sometimes, it's best to think of these data points as being interesting, but other times they can serve as a spark to nudge your business in the right direction.

How do you tell the difference? Common sense plays a role, obviously, but so does repetition. If you find that many web visitors are pointing at the same ideas, you can pick up on a trend before your competitors are able to spot it.

Look For Ways To Grow And Optimize

Your web-based startup should always be growing and evolving, and your web analytics package can point the way. What we're really talking about here is optimizing your website so that you're always generating more traffic, more conversions, and a stronger base of business.

There's an old saying: "The numbers don't lie." That's never been more true than it is now in the digital age. There are a million different ways to grow and strengthen your company, if you're only willing to pay attention to what customers "tell" you through their actions.

Where some business owners see confusion in web analytics, others see opportunity. The more you acquaint yourself with web performance statistics, the easier it is going to be to figure out where there's room for growth, which sections of your website need improvement, and how to carry your startup to the next level of profitability.

20 | Your Recruiting Starts Online

At a certain point, any successful business is likely to grow to the point where additional employees are needed to help keep things moving forward. Based on your concept, that might be early on, or it could come later after you've found some success in the market.

As any experienced business owner can tell you, hiring the right employees can make or break your company. Whether they are hourly support staff or full-time managers, you need personnel who can take your vision and translate it to every task or customer interaction.

Not surprisingly, the recruiting for a web-based startup should begin on the website itself. So let's take a brief look at what you can do to pull in the right kinds of men and women to put your company on the right path...

Post Your Job Listings On Your Website

Unless you have immediate openings that have to be filled before your website can go live, consider posting new openings on your website instead of traditional job boards. Assuming you get a decent amount of traffic, taking this approach gives you an instant benefit: You are likely to draw in applicants who are already familiar with your business (and industry) like you, and want to be a part of a startup.

These might not seem like huge advantages, when compared to normal résumé qualifications, but they can make all the difference between hiring someone who is committed to your business and bringing in a warm body that will have to be replaced later. Recruiting is about so much more than matching skills and qualifications – you should be looking for the right person with a personality and vision that match up well with your future, not just a matching schedule and salary requirements.

Make Your Company's Personality Shine Through

On the other side of things, business owners tend to think that employees just want a job that pays them the most money while requiring the fewest hours. There's certainly a grain of truth in that, but you'll have a much, much easier time attracting top talent to your company if your business has a discernible personality.

Although this ties back to earlier thoughts on marketing, it's hard to overstate the importance of standing out. Very few people are ever satisfied with "just another job" at "just another company." If you can show them a way to have fun, feel good about what they do, and be part of a venture that is just taking off, you can win their loyalty.

This will come through in their productivity, as well as the way they treat your customers and think about their future. If you want to hire the best, and keep them, inspire them with the story and vision behind your startup.

Be The Right Kind Of Employer

As you take on new team members, treat them more like partners than staff. That's good advice for almost any management setting, but particularly in a brand-new company.

In the same way that you have to prove yourself to customers, you may have to "sell" your concept to potential employees who are considering multiple opportunities and/or job offers. By having your current employees stick up for you, you increase the odds that their friends and colleagues will want to come and join forces, as well.

What we're really talking about here is being the kind of employer the best employees love, and then building your reputation – just as you would with customers – so that people want to come and work with or for you. Being known as the kind of company that builds people up, highlights their successes, and treats them like the heart and soul of an enterprise is the most powerful recruiting advantage you can ever give yourself. And once again, the better you become at recruiting, the stronger your new business gets.

As you work through the plan to create your web-based startup, recruiting might not be one of your big concerns or priorities. Remember, however, that like marketing, hiring the right people can have a huge impact and steer you toward success or failure. And so, with that in mind, it makes sense to think about where your business might expand going forward, and how you can use your web presence to draw in the right kinds of candidates.

21 | Be Ready To Grow And Adapt Your Startup

If you gain nothing else from this book, I hope you'll walk away with the idea that starting a successful web-based company is about having a great concept and executing it through the right principles. Those principles – such as knowing your customer base, providing something new, and reaching out to buyers in a way that's efficient – don't change. They are as old as time.

Specific tactics and strategies, however, do change on a regular basis. So too might the business plan behind your startup, the opportunities that are in front of you, or even the monetization of your product or service.

In other words, it's highly likely that you and your business will both need to grow and adapt over time. Otherwise, you'll find yourself in a position where you've become stale, outdated, irrelevant, or passed up by a competitor who is more innovative.

Being adaptable is more about a particular mindset than it is a specific set of actions, but here are a few things you should think about along the way...

Nothing Is Ever Set In Stone

It's easy to fall in love with a particular product, business model, website design, or other element of your business. And yet, the moment you do, you become attached to something that might have to be changed or shifted later.

Online, entire companies can shift and transform overnight. While it's hard to even imagine now, there was a time when Amazon only sold books over the Internet and e-readers were virtually unheard of. Had they clung to that philosophy, the company would be a shadow of what it is today. eBay started out as a simple auction concept, but changed to incorporate different stores, categories, and even vehicles. And of course, the company spawned the popular PayPal brand, which revolutionized online payments.

These kinds of shifts were only possible because entrepreneurs and executives realized that the world is always changing and there aren't any details that should ever be accepted as a definite fact of life. If you can remember that nothing about your business is set in stone, you'll be primed to grow and adjust as needed.

Follow The Market

Sometimes, deciding to change your business model isn't much of a choice at all. Occasionally, the market – or even an individual competitor – will take you there on their own.

For an obvious example, let's go back to the earlier point I made about Amazon. In the early days of the company, competing businesses (like Barnes & Noble) could get by with retail stores. Before long, though, these companies were forced to adapt and produce e-readers of their own. And of course the ones that didn't have now closed their doors.

The lesson to be learned here is that sometimes you have to follow your market. It's better to be in the lead position and dictating terms to other businesses, but when that isn't possible, don't ignore the obvious. Keep up with the times, and you won't find yourself on the outside of your own industry looking in.

Look For Innovation Anywhere You Can Find It

Innovation is a mindset, not an act, and it can be discovered anywhere. It goes without saying that you should keep an eye on your competitors to see what they are up to, and whether they have ideas or concepts you should be adopting in your own business (and expect they'll do the same to you).

At the same time, you also want to look for creative thinking and new solutions in other businesses. Any practice or idea you come across that changes the way things are done, or makes life easier for customers, can potentially be utilized within your own company.

Innovation comes from every discipline and corner of life. The better you can get at spotting it and learning from what you see, the easier it will be to keep your startup on the cutting edge after your business "grows up."

Pay Attention To Vendors And Customers

Occasionally, good ideas to improve your web-based business will be presented to you on a silver platter. How? By suggestions being made through vendors or customers.

In the case of customers, good ideas come because they already know what they want, and may have a perspective that's much different than your own. Your vendors, conversely, should know a bit about your company and their own respective fields.

Accountants, IT professionals, and business consultants are all obvious examples of places you can look to for innovation and bottom-line improvement. The only trick to making them work is that you have to be open to listening and examining different thoughts to see whether they fit in your business plan.

Prioritize Opportunity Over Fear

Finding and developing a profitable concept for an online business isn't easy. There's so much risk and chance in the beginning that some entrepreneurs can begin to cling to any sign of early success, afraid to make any changes that might cause them to lose what they've gotten.

That's natural and sensible, but it isn't a good way to run your company. If you want to stay in business, much less keep growing, you have to hold on to the attitude that helped you launch your startup in the first place. That is, you have to prioritize future opportunities over current fears and worries.

Change is a constant, both online and in the business world. So when you bring the two together, it's only natural that you're going to have to keep shifting and evolving to adjust to market conditions.

Conclusion:
Are You Ready To Get Moving On Your Startup Concept?

If you reach this point in the book, then you are very likely serious about turning your inspiration into an actual working, profitable web-based startup. That's a great feeling, and I'm very excited on your behalf.

At the same time, you might be feeling equal parts enthralled and overwhelmed. Even in this short overview, there's a lot to take in. Many new clients come to my company without a deep understanding of what it actually takes to start and run a successful company. There are more steps and factors to consider than a lot of people realize.

My advice would be this: Remember that it's entirely possible to build a successful startup from the ground up, provided you get the right help and take everything step by step. Don't lose sight of your vision, but don't rush through the process and skip over important points or details, either.

I'm certainly not going to be the one to tell you that it's easy to build a profitable startup from nothing, but I know from experience that it's entirely possible, too. With the right idea, a bit of commitment, and some expert advice, you can absolutely turn your dream into a reality. And you can change a whole industry – not to mention your own life – along the way.

So while I can certainly teach you a lot about what it takes to get your business moving, the one thing I can't answer is the most important question of them all: *Are you ready to get moving on your startup concept?*

Note that this isn't the same as asking whether you want to own a successful company. Almost everyone desires that. Unfortunately, many aren't willing to put in the hard work, do the research needed, or think creatively enough to make it happen.

Only you know whether the determination is in you. If it is, then your idea can be refined and honed into something that's going to work. If you don't have the right attitude, though, no amount of reading, coaching, or investment is going to fix the problem.

Never forget that a web-based startup is a wonderful thing. New companies create jobs, drive change, and turn dreams into realities. And in the digital age, it's easier (and less expensive) than ever to begin your own business with little more than a good idea. But if you aren't willing to work to make your idea into the one that others point to as a success story later, then you're really signing up for an expensive hobby... and one that isn't likely to pay big dividends in the future.

Whatever your vision for the future is, you can make it with a web-based startup. Just be sure you start out with the right mindset, because it's going to take a bit of work and perseverance before you can become an "overnight success."

Best of luck – I look forward to seeing your creation online soon!

Paul J. Scott is the founder and president of GoingClear Interactive, a Boston-based web design and web development firm.

Entrepreneurial from a young age, Paul got his "big break" in the business world caddying for influential business leaders as a teenager in Nantucket. He carried the lessons learned from those encounters into the corporate world, where he got his professional start managing websites and advertising for a large publishing company.

In 2001, Paul decided to launch his own business, GoingClear Interactive, by working evenings and weekends in a shared studio space. A focus on creative thinking, client service, and commonsense solutions helped to grow the company quickly, and the firm is now considered a leader in custom web development. Today, GoingClear Interactive works with businesses, nonprofits, universities, and government agencies of all sizes, helping them to make the most of web programming and their websites.

A Boston native, Paul is a graduate of Bentley University and holds a master's certificate in web development and e-commerce from Clark University. When he's not finding new ways to make websites work, he enjoys spending time with his family, motorcycling, learning yoga, training in Krav Maga, volunteering for the Big Brothers program, golfing, and other activities.

You can learn more about Paul and his company GoingClear Interactive at GoingClear.com.